DATE

GRAPHIC MYTHOLOGY

AFRICAN MYTHS

by Gary Jeffrey

illustrated by Terry Riley

The Rosen Publishing Group, Inc., New York

Published in 2006 by The Rosen Publishing Group, Inc.
29 East 21st Street, New York, NY 10010
Copyright © 2006 David West Books

First edition, 2006

Designed and produced by
David West Books

Editor: Charlotte Cattermole

Photo credits:
    Page 5 top, Peeter Viisimaa

Library of Congress Cataloging-in-Publication Data

Jeffrey, Gary.
    African myths / by Gary Jeffrey ; illustrated by Terry Riley.
    p. cm. -- (Graphic mythology)
    Includes index.
    ISBN 1-4042-0798-8 (lib. bdg.) -- ISBN 1-4042-0810-0 (pbk.) -- ISBN 1-4042-6250-4 (6 pack)
    1. Mythology, Sub-Saharan African. I Title. II. Series.

    BL2462.5.J44 2005
    299.6'113--dc22

                                                            2005017642

Manufactured in China

CONTENTS

ORIGINS

Africa is an enormous continent, over three times the size of the United States. It is divided by the huge Sahara desert. Very little is known about the ancient civilizations that existed south of the Sahara because there was no written culture before the nineteenth century.

THE SPOKEN TRADITION

The ancient Africans loved to tell stories and sing songs. This oral storytelling has given us the African myths we know today. West Africa is home to hundreds of different tribes, whose customs and beliefs shift and change over time. Between the Senegal and Congo rivers alone, there are more than two thousand languages. Because of this rich variety of storytellers, there are often many different versions of the same tale.

The Chagga of Tanzania are a group made up of various African tribes who settled by Mount Kilimanjaro hundreds of years ago. Their myths come from their agricultural way of life.

A TREASURY OF STORIES

Storytelling took place at the the end of the day when the work was done. Why did people tell stories? Some stories came from the human need to find meaning in everyday life. Other tales were meant to make the listener think about the faults of humans. Meanwhile others were invented simply to delight and entertain. Although characters varied depending on the location, many African myths had similar story lines.

The ancient people of Dahomey (now Benin) believed the leopard to be an ancient relative of their kings. Masks such as the one on the right were worn to honor them.

GODS, TRICKSTERS, AND ANIMALS

Legends that explain creation, trickster stories with a sting in the tail, and moral fables involving talking animals have been handed down for generations. Stories about the gods explain how things came to be. Trickster tales feature characters who use their wits to upset social order or overcome a stronger rival, often for their own amusement. In other fables, man comes to depend on the help of talking animals to complete a quest.

The trickster could be a spider, tortoise, or hare. The hare is a popular character throughout Central and East Africa.

THREE AFRICAN MYTHS

These tales, taken from different regions of the continent, are typical African stories that explore basic themes about creation, existence, and being smarter than your enemies!

THE STORY OF CREATION

This story explains how the world was formed by the gods, as understood by the ancient Yoruban civilization from a region in West Africa that is now part of Nigeria. It also explains how human beings came to exist and survive on Earth.

Olorun
The wisest of the sky gods, he is the supreme ruler. The creator of the sun, Olorun eventually gives life to man.

Obatala
An adventurous and clever young sky god whose interest in Earth and belief in his own ideas set the story in motion.

Orunmila
The eldest son of Olorun, he is the chief Diviner and can tell the future. He is also widely known by the name Ifa.

Olokun
Goddess of the sea and marshes, Olokun is a powerful, fiery, and passionate deity as well as a highly skilled weaver.

How Anansi Came to Own all the Tales that are Told

Anansi is the famous spider who uses his knowledge and quick thinking to trick larger creatures and even the gods. Although his actions can sometimes be naughty, Anansi is a character held in great affection by Africans all over the world.

Nyame
The sky god of the Ashanti people, Nyame is leader of the gods. He was the first to own all the stories in the world.

Anansi
An intelligent and sneaky spider who likes to trick others. His love of telling stories leads him on an adventure.

Onini
The wise and strong python of the forest and a character not easily tricked.

Osebo
The strong and powerful leopard who one would be smart not to anger.

The Story of Dog and Jackal

This story tells how the dog became man's best friend. Animal fables like this make an entertaining tale by explaining how everyday things started to happen.

Dog
A very clever animal, Dog is tired of life in the wilderness.

Jackal
As tough and sly as a fox, Jackal loves the freedom of the wild.

Man
He lives near Dog and Jackal in a village that has food and warmth.

THE STORY OF CREATION

From the Yoruba people of
West Africa

IN THE BEGINNING, THERE EXISTED ONLY
SKY AND A VAST EMPTY OCEAN.

THE SKY WAS PEOPLED BY MANY GODS
OR "ORISHA." THEIR RULER WAS
OLORUN, THE WISEST OF THEM ALL.

IN THE SEA BELOW WAS A POWERFUL
GODDESS, OLOKUN. OLOKUN LIVED
ALONE. SHE HAD A BAD TEMPER.

THE SKY AND SEA WERE NOT
REALLY INTERESTED IN EACH
OTHER. THE ORISHA IN THE
CLOUDS GENERALLY IGNORED
THE GRAY WATER AND
LIFELESS MARSHES
BENEATH THEM.

ORUNMILA WAS OLORUN'S ELDEST SON AND THE ORISHA OF DIVINATION, OR TELLING THE FUTURE.

OBATALA! I'VE BEEN EXPECTING YOU!

I KNOW OF YOUR PLAN. SIT DOWN WHILE I THROW THE NUTS.

SIXTEEN PALM NUTS WERE THROWN ONTO THE DIVINING TRAY OVER AND OVER AGAIN.

ORUNMILA READ THE DIFFERENT MEANINGS.

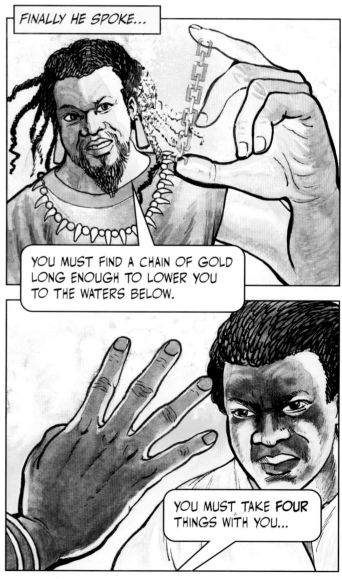

FINALLY HE SPOKE...

YOU MUST FIND A CHAIN OF GOLD LONG ENOUGH TO LOWER YOU TO THE WATERS BELOW.

YOU MUST TAKE FOUR THINGS WITH YOU...

A HORN OF SAND...

A WHITE HEN...

A BLACK CAT FOR COMPANY...

AND A PALM NUT.

OBATALA THANKED ORUNMILA AND WENT TO SEE THE GOLDSMITH.

I WILL HAPPILY MAKE A CHAIN IF YOU CAN FIND ENOUGH GOLD TO MAKE IT **WITH!**

I WILL FIND THE GOLD. **YOU** BEGIN THE WORK!

OBATALA WENT TO ASK THE OTHER ORISHA FOR HELP. THEY OFFERED HIM ALL THE GOLD THEY HAD.

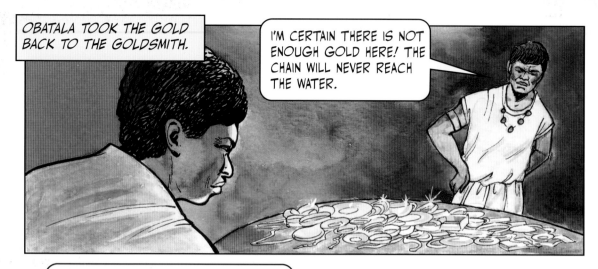

OBATALA TOOK THE GOLD BACK TO THE GOLDSMITH.

I'M CERTAIN THERE IS NOT ENOUGH GOLD HERE! THE CHAIN WILL NEVER REACH THE WATER.

THIS WAS ALL I COULD GET! **MAKE** THE CHAIN AND WHEN IT IS FINISHED, ATTACH A STRONG **HOOK** TO ONE END.

FINALLY, THE GOLD CHAIN WAS READY. OBATALA STOOD AT THE EDGE OF THE SKY.

ORUNMILA APPEARED...

HERE ARE THE THINGS YOU WILL NEED.

I AM READY TO GO!

AS HE LOWERED HIMSELF DOWN, THE LIGHT SLOWLY FADED INTO DARKNESS. SOON HE REACHED THE END OF THE CHAIN...

THERE IS NOTHING BUT MIST BELOW. I CAN **HEAR** THE WATER, BUT IF I DROP NOW I WILL LAND **RIGHT IN IT!**

A VOICE CAME FROM ABOVE...

OBATALA!

LAND QUICKLY SPREAD OUT AROUND THE HEN. RIVERS AND VALLEYS SOON FORMED.

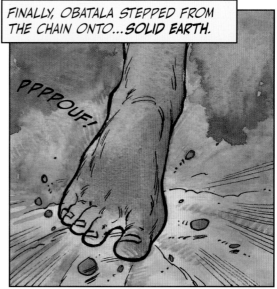

FINALLY, OBATALA STEPPED FROM THE CHAIN ONTO...**SOLID EARTH.**

PPPPOUF!

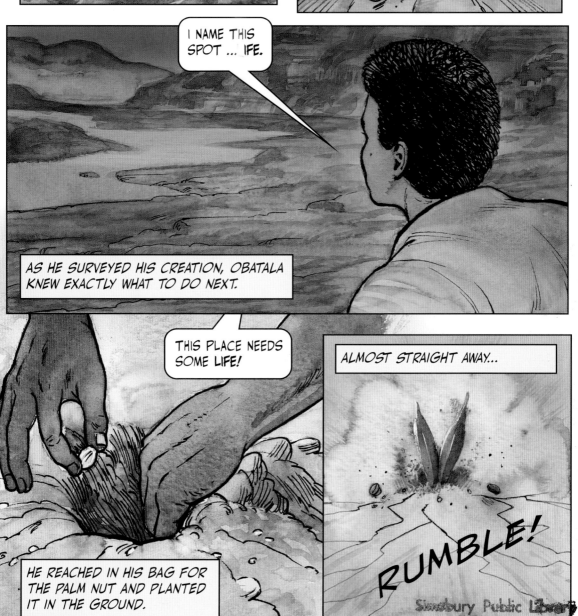

I NAME THIS SPOT ... IFE.

AS HE SURVEYED HIS CREATION, OBATALA KNEW EXACTLY WHAT TO DO NEXT.

THIS PLACE NEEDS SOME **LIFE!**

ALMOST STRAIGHT AWAY...

RUMBLE!

HE REACHED IN HIS BAG FOR THE PALM NUT AND PLANTED IT IN THE GROUND.

15

OLORUN
CONCENTRATED...

...AND CREATED A SUN. HE SENT IT DOWN TO LIGHT THE EARTH.

THAT IS MUCH BETTER!

BUT CAT, THERE IS STILL SOMETHING **MISSING** FROM THIS PLACE...

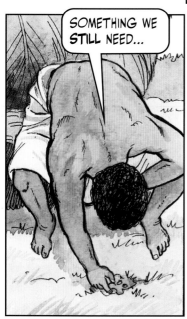

SOMETHING WE **STILL** NEED...

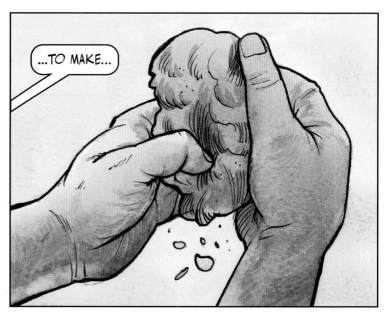

...TO MAKE...

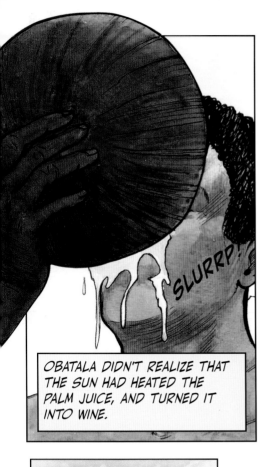

SLURRP!

OBATALA DIDN'T REALIZE THAT THE SUN HAD HEATED THE PALM JUICE, AND TURNED IT INTO WINE.

THE WINE MADE HIS HEAD SPIN.

NOW, BACK TO WORK!

THUNK!

STUMBLE!

HIS FINGERS BECAME CLUMSY.

THE FIGURES HE MADE WERE BADLY FORMED AND DISTORTED.

BUT HE CARRIED ON UNTIL AT LAST...

THAT'S IT. I HAVE MADE ENOUGH!

OBATALA HAD DONE A LOT, BUT HE FELT TIRED AND HOMESICK. HE DECIDED TO RETURN TO THE SKY.

WHEN HE ARRIVED...

OBATALA, WE HAVE HEARD MANY RUMORS ABOUT THE GREAT LAND YOU HAVE CREATED **BELOW**!

YOU MUST TELL US ALL ABOUT IT!

THE ORISHA WERE ENTRANCED BY OBATALA'S TALES OF HIS CREATION. MANY DECIDED TO LEAVE THE HEAVENS AND LIVE ON THE EARTH. AS THEY GOT READY TO LEAVE, OBATALA CALLED THEM TOGETHER...

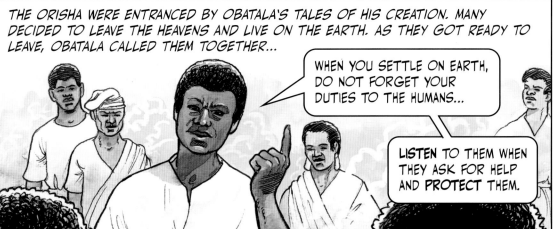

WHEN YOU SETTLE ON EARTH, DO NOT FORGET YOUR DUTIES TO THE HUMANS...

LISTEN TO THEM WHEN THEY ASK FOR HELP AND **PROTECT** THEM.

THE ORISHA CLIMBED DOWN THE CHAIN.

ONCE ON EARTH, THEY BEGAN DIVIDING UP THE LAND BETWEEN THEM. HUMANS WELCOMED THEM WITH OPEN ARMS.

MEANWHILE, SOMEONE ELSE WAS NOT FEELING QUITE SO HAPPY...

WHEN OBATALA HEARD ABOUT THE DEVASTATION, HE BECAME VERY WORRIED.

...BUT I'M NOT REALLY SURE HOW TO HANDLE OLOKUN.

HE CONSULTED WITH ORUNMILA.

THE PALM NUTS SAY YOU SHOULD REST HERE, OBATALA. IT IS MY TURN TO GO DOWN TO EARTH.

ORUNMILA CLIMBED DOWN THE CHAIN AND USED HIS GREAT POWERS TO TURN BACK THE RAGING WATERS.

HE STOPPED THE FLOODS. THE LAND BECAME VISIBLE AGAIN. OLOKUN WAS **DEFEATED.**

THE GRATEFUL PEOPLE RETURNED TO IFE. ORUNMILA PREPARED TO LEAVE.

ORUNMILA, STAY AND PROTECT US!

I HAVE TO GO. OLORUN NEEDS ME! BUT I WILL TEACH YOU HOW TO PROTECT **YOURSELVES.**

ORUNMILA TAUGHT HUMANS THE ART OF DIVINING SO THAT THEY WOULD BE ABLE TO PREDICT THE ACTIONS OF NATURE'S FORCES.

HOW ANANSI CAME TO OWN
ALL THE TALES THAT ARE TOLD

From the Ashanti people of Ghana

ALL THE STORIES IN THE WORLD BELONGED TO THE SKY GOD NYAME. KWAKU ANANSI, THE SPIDER, HAD *LONG* WANTED TO OWN THEM. ONE DAY, HE WENT TO SEE NYAME AND OFFERED TO BUY THE STORIES FROM HIM...

I'M HAPPY TO SELL YOU MY STORIES ANANSI. BUT YOU MUST KNOW, THE PRICE IS HIGH.

MANY RICH AND POWERFUL PEOPLE HAVE TRIED TO BUY THEM BUT COULD NOT MATCH THE ASKING PRICE. DO YOU THINK YOU CAN DO IT?

I CAN. WHAT IS THE PRICE?

ANANSI POSITIONED HIMSELF OVER MMOBORO'S NEST. HE FLICKED SOME WATER ON HIMSELF AND SPRINKLED THE REST ON THE NEST.

YOU FOOLISH CREATURES! WHY DO YOU STAY IN THAT FRAGILE NEST WHEN THE GREAT RAINS HAVE ALREADY BEGUN?

BUT ANANSI, WHERE SHALL WE GO?

GO IN HERE...THIS DRY GOURD WILL PROTECT YOU FROM THE STORMS.

ZZZZZZZZZZZZZZZZZZZZZZZT!

OH! BUT YOU REALLY ARE FOOLISH CREATURES!

THANK YOU, ANANSI!

ZZZZT!

PLUG!

ANANSI TOOK MMOBORO TO THE SKY GOD.

VERY GOOD, ANANSI...

...BUT THERE ARE STILL **TWO** MORE THINGS.

ANANSI RETURNED TO THE FOREST. HE CUT A LARGE BAMBOO POLE AND SOME LENGTHS OF STRONG VINE.

HACK!

THEN HE WALKED PAST ONINI'S HOUSE TALKING LOUDLY TO HIMSELF.

...MY WIFE IS VERY SILLY — SHE SAYS HE IS **SHORTER** AND **WEAKER**, BUT I SAY HE IS **LONGER** AND **STRONGER**. SHE GIVES HIM **LESS** RESPECT, I GIVE HIM **MORE**! WHO IS RIGHT?

HEY YOU! WHY ARE YOU ARGUING WITH YOURSELF?

I HAVE HAD A DISAGREEMENT WITH MY WIFE. SHE SAYS YOU ARE SHORTER AND WEAKER THAN THIS POLE. I THINK YOU ARE LONGER AND STRONGER.

THERE IS NO SENSE IN ARGUING WHEN WE CAN EASILY FIND OUT THE TRUTH. I WILL LIE DOWN, AND WE CAN MEASURE WITH THE STICK.

ANANSI LAID DOWN THE POLE.

YOU SEEM A LITTLE SHORT. CAN YOU STRETCH AT ALL?

OK.

A BIT MORE PLEASE.

I CAN'T STRETCH ANY MORE!

THIS IS VERY ODD. WHEN YOU STRETCH AT ONE END, THE OTHER END SHRINKS.

ONINI AGREED. THEN ANANSI QUICKLY TIED HIS HEAD TO THE POLE AND WRAPPED THE REST OF THE VINE AROUND HIS BODY.

I KNOW. WHY DON'T I TIE YOUR HEAD TO THE POLE TO STOP YOU FROM SLIPPING?

THE GREAT PYTHON WAS **TRAPPED!**

ONINI, MY WIFE WAS RIGHT. YOU **ARE** SHORTER AND WEAKER THAN THE POLE. WHAT'S MORE, YOU ARE FOOLISH, TOO!

ANANSI TOOK HIS PRISONER TO NYAME. BUT THERE WAS STILL ONE LAST THING TO GET...

...BACK IN THE FOREST, ANANSI DUG A DEEP HOLE ON OSEBO'S FAVORITE PATH.

SCOOP!

THEN HE CAREFULLY COVERED THE OPENING WITH BRANCHES, LEAVES, AND DIRT.

NOW, ALL I HAVE TO DO IS WAIT.

NIGHT FELL AND OSEBO CAME PROWLING.

AH...OSEBO, YOU ARE HALF-FOOLISH!

YEEEOOOOW!

CRASH!

IN THE MORNING, ANANSI LOOKED IN.

OSEBO, WHAT **ARE** YOU DOING IN THERE?

I'VE FALLEN INTO THIS TRAP. HELP ME OUT!

I'D LIKE TO HELP YOU, BUT I FEAR IF I DO, YOU WILL EAT ME, MY WIFE, AND ALL MY CHILDREN!

I PROMISE I WONT!

OK. SINCE YOU'VE PROMISED, I **WILL** HELP YOU.

AND WITH THAT, ANANSI CLIMBED TO THE TOP OF A NEARBY TREE.

THE LEOPARD STRUGGLED HARD BUT COULD NOT BREAK FREE. ANANSI KILLED HIM WITH HIS KNIFE.

THAK!

HE CARRIED HIS PRIZE TO THE SKY GOD.

KWAKU ANANSI, YOU HAVE DONE WHAT ALL THE GREAT **WARRIORS AND CHIEFS** WERE UNABLE TO DO. YOU HAVE PAID THE PRICE!

HERE ARE MY STORIES. NOW THEY BELONG TO **YOU.**

FROM THIS DAY ONWARD, WHENEVER SOMEONE TELLS A STORY HE OR SHE MUST REMEMBER ANANSI.

FOR IT IS TO ANANSI THE SPIDER THAT ALL TALES BELONG.

THE END

36

THE STORY OF DOG
AND JACKAL

From the Bushongo people of Zaire

IN ANCIENT TIMES, DOG AND JACKAL LIVED SIDE BY SIDE, LIKE BROTHERS.

THEY HUNTED TOGETHER...

...SHARED THEIR KILLS.

LIFE WAS GOOD. THEY HAD NEVER GONE HUNGRY FOR MORE THAN TWO DAYS.

BUT ALL THAT WAS ABOUT TO CHANGE...

HE SPOTTED A SECOND BONE.

GNNARGH!

THEN...

YOU MUST BE WARMED UP BY **NOW?**

PLEASE, JUST A FEW MINUTES MORE!

OK. NOW I WILL GO TO SLEEP. BUT WHEN I WAKE UP, YOU **MUST** BE GONE!

FINALLY, DOG LAY DOWN. HE FELL ASLEEP.

HOURS PASSED...

43

MORE MYTHICAL CHARACTERS

Originating from many different tribes and places, African mythology is a treasure chest of colorful, larger-than-life characters. Here is a small sample of heroes, kings, and gods.

GIHILIHILI (THE SNAKE-MAN) – A character from a Rwandan fable in which a woman gives birth to a snake that sheds its skin and changes into a man. The man wishes to marry the local chief's daughter, but his family is poor. So he throws his old snake skin on the fire where it magically changes into the gifts he needs to offer the chief.

IMANA – The god of the Tutsi people from Rwanda, Imana is the only god they believe in. He is the creator of all things. He planned to save mankind from death, but when he tried to catch death, a woman hid it from him, and he became angry. This is why mankind is not immortal.

KIANDA – A demon from traditional tales of Angola, where demons are considered to be like gods and demand gifts and sacrifices from the people. Kianda rules over the water.

KINTU – A king of Uganda, Kintu was thought to be an immortal descendant of the gods, and often visited the creator deity, Katonda, to tell him about mankind's progress on Earth.

LEGBA – A trickster god who originated with the Fon of Dahomey (Benin). Legba, the youngest child of Mawu-Lisa, understands all languages. In special ceremonies, he acts as a messenger between the human and spirit worlds.

LIONGO – A character from the Swahili people of Zanzibar, Liongo is said to have been a real person. His story is greatly admired by the people. Liongo was an extremely powerful man who terrorized the people in his city until they tried to capture him. He was eventually killed by one of his relatives.

MAWU-LISA – The chief god of the Fon of Dahomey (Benin) who has two faces. Mawu, the female face, controls the moon. The other face is her husband, Lisa, who controls the sun. Mawu-Lisa created the universe and gave birth to the seven children who rule the Earth. The youngest child is Legba.

NZAMBI – Nzambi is a god of the Bacongo people of Angola. He is associated with the sun. He is also very powerful and smart. He is the creator of individuals. He gives them different tastes and varied personalities.

SHANGO – Shango is the god of thunder, and is also an ancestor of the Yoruba people. He is often shown with a double axe on his head, the symbol of thunder, and six eyes. Shango has three wives. His symbolic animal is the ram (a male sheep).

SHEBA – A historical figure who also appears in Ethiopian myths, and in Christian and Islamic stories. Sheba was a queen named Makeda, who was to be sacrificed to the serpent-king, Arwe. Arwe is killed but as he dies, a drop of his blood falls onto Makeda's foot and changes it into a donkey's hoof. She then becomes the queen of Sheba and travels to see Solomon with the hope that he can heal her.

UMKXAKAZA-WAKOGINGQWAYO – The heroine of an epic tale of the Zulu people of South Africa, she was the daughter of a king. Her name comes from the description of an army going into battle. She was taken from her village by a giant beast, and was then taken by a tribe who wanted to eat her. After many adventures, she managed to return home.

GLOSSARY

agriculture The practice of farming land and raising animals.

banish To force someone to leave a place as a form of punishment.

barren Empty of anything.

calabash A container made from a gourd.

deity A god, goddess, or extremely powerful being.

devastate To destroy or ruin something.

disability A lack of fitness, power, or ability in body or mind.

distort To twist into a strange shape.

diviner Someone who can look into the future.

entranced To be completely fascinated and interested in something.

epic A long story telling the actions of a legendary or historical hero.

fable A story that teaches a lesson.

goldsmith A person who works with and makes things from gold.

gourd A hard-skinned fruit that cannot be eaten but is used as
    a container.

hare A fast-moving animal, much like a rabbit, but with larger ears
    and longer back legs.

harmony A state of agreement and understanding.

hornets Large wasps that have powerful stings.

immortal Can live forever.

jackal A wild member of the dog family.

lair The home of a wild animal.

malformed Distorted and misshapen.

predict To say that something is going to happen, before it has.

prowl To move about in a secretive way, like a hunter.

revenge An act of getting even with someone.

sacrifice To offer up a gift to a god, often as a way of making peace.

shamed Feeling embarrassed.

trickster A person or character who deliberately cheats and
    misleads others.

weave To form cloth by braiding together strands of thread.

Yoruba People from a certain tribe in Nigeria. There are almost 10
    million of the Yoruba people.

FOR MORE INFORMATION

ORGANIZATIONS

Museum for African Art
36-01 43rd Avenue at 36th Street
Long Island City, NY 11101
(718) 784-7700
Web Site: http://www.africanart.org

Worcester African Cultural Center
33 Canterbury Street
Worcester, MA 01610
(508) 757-7727
Web Site: http://www.african-museum.com

FOR FURTHER READING

Ardagh, Philip. *African Myths and Legends*. Chicago, IL: World Book Inc., 2001.

Arnott, Kathleen. *African Myths and Legends*. Oxford: Oxford University Press, 1990.

Bellingham, David. *The Kingfisher Book of Mythology: Gods, Goddesses and Heroes From Around the World*. London: Kingfisher Publications, Plc., 2001.

Lily, Melinda. *Warrior Son of a Warrior Son*: A Masai Tale. Vero Beach, FL: Rourke Publishing, 1998.

Philip, Neil. *The Illustrated Book of Myths: Tales and Legends of the World*. London, England: Dorling Kinderlsey Limited, 1995.

Washington, Donna L. *A Pride of African Tales*. Los Angeles, CA: Amistad, 2004.

INDEX

Web Sites

Due to the changing nature of Internet links, the Rosen Publishing Group, Inc., has developed an online list of Web sites related to the subject of this book. This site is updated regularly. Please use this link to access the list:

http://www.rosenlinks.com/gm/african